DD	DV	LB	BR
6/09			
DL	DW	BO	BT
DM	DX	LM	

My Parents' Divorce

© Aladdin Books Ltd 2007

Designed and produced by
Aladdin Books Ltd
2/3 Fitzroy Mews
London W1T 6DF

First published in 2007
in Great Britain
by Franklin Watts
338 Euston Road
London NW1 3BH

Franklin Watts Australia
Level 17/207 Kent Street
Sydney NSW 2000

Franklin Watts is a division of Hachette Children's Books.

ISBN 978 0 7496 7498 4

A catalogue record for
this book is available
from the British Library.

Illustrator: Christopher O'Neill

The author, Julia Cole, is a trained counsellor and one of the UK's best-known
relationship experts. She writes and broadcasts regularly on relationship issues.

Dewey Classification:
306.89

My Parents' Divorce

Julia Cole

Aladdin/Watts

London • Sydney

Contents

Introduction

The children in this book know how it feels when a mum and dad decide to live apart. You may have a friend whose parents are separated or divorced, or your parents may have split up. Join the children in this book as they talk about their feelings.

I live with my mum and see my dad at weekends.

My mum and dad are separated. I live with my dad.

My parents are getting a divorce.

Mum and Dad divorced when I was a baby. I live with my mum, but I see my dad all the time.

What Is Divorce?

Adam is explaining to Leon that separation is when two grown-ups who have lived together decide to live apart. If they are married they may also decide to get a divorce. You may hear someone say that his or her parents have split up. This can mean that they are separated or divorced.

Splitting up is when parents separate. It's also when parents divorce.

What is the difference between divorce and separation?

Grown-ups can only divorce if they are married. They may separate first.

▶ Splitting Up

Splitting up is when grown-ups decide to live apart. If they are married, they may decide to divorce. Grown-ups who split up usually live in separate homes. They may live alone or they may live with a new partner.

◀ Who Gets Divorced?

Only grown-ups who have been married can get a divorce, because a divorce is a legal end to a marriage. But grown-ups who are married can still separate without getting a divorce. However, even though parents are divorcing each other, they are *not* divorcing their children.

▶ A Hard Decision

It's not easy for a husband and wife to decide to end their marriage. They may spend a long time trying to solve their problems before they realise they just can't fix them.

If parents have been fighting a lot, some children may even feel relieved that they are divorcing.

Adam, tell us about your parents.

"My parents split up about four years ago. I don't see my dad any more. I live with my mum. Because my mum and dad never married, they didn't need to get a divorce. I don't think it matters if you call it divorce, separation or splitting up. They all mean that two grown-ups have decided to live separately."

What Happens?

My dad is looking for somewhere else to live.

Dad and I moved to a new house.

We've decided to live apart.

One parent usually moves out.

You don't have to split up!

Alice is telling Lily that her dad is going to live somewhere else. When Lily's parents split up, she and her dad moved house. Each situation is different, but most mums and dads want to make sure their children will be OK. Whatever your mum and dad do, you will still be looked after.

Story: Staying Friends

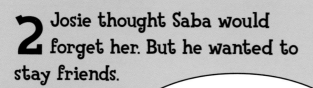

1 Saba thought divorce or separation happened straight away.

> Why do your parents still live together if they are divorcing?

> Because my dad is looking for a new house for us to live in.

> It means that I'll have to move school as well.

2 Josie thought Saba would forget her. But he wanted to stay friends.

> Maybe you could come and stay at my house in the holidays.

> When Mum and Dad separated we stayed in our house and Dad moved out.

3 Talking helped Josie and Saba to realise that each situation is different.

Why is it different for Saba and Josie?

Saba and Josie now know that every family is different. One parent may move out before you have been told what is happening. Or your parents may tell you that they are splitting up before anything happens. Like Saba you may stay in your home, or like Josie you may have to move house.

▶ What About Me?

Sometimes your parents will decide between themselves whom you stay with or they may ask you what you think. Sometimes the courts need to help decide this. They may also decide when and if you see your other parent.

Can he live with us in our new house?

◀ Together Again!

The parent from whom you live apart may try to visit or to see you as much as he or she can. However, this may not always be possible. You can ask the parent with whom you live to explain the new situation.

▶ A Parent Forever

After your parents divorce you will usually live with only one parent for most of the time. But the parent who lives somewhere else is still your Mum or Dad. They won't stop loving you.

It's not fair. I want to live with both of you.

Story: Does She Love Me?

1 Sam wanted her mum and dad to stay together, but her mum was moving out.

2 Sam's parents had decided that Sam would stay with her dad.

It's better for you to stay with your dad for the moment.

Just because I don't live with you doesn't mean that I don't love you. You'll see me at weekends.

3 Sam found it difficult to understand how her mum could leave and still love her.

Will Sam's mum still love her?

Sam's mum is going to live apart from Sam and her dad, but this doesn't mean that she will stop loving Sam. She will still see Sam regularly. Some parents stay in contact with their children a lot. Others don't visit very much, but whatever happens, they will always be your mum and dad.

Alice, you live with your dad now. Do you see your mum?
"Yes. When my parents separated they decided that my sister, Nicole, and I should live with Dad. We moved house and everything. But Nicole and I still see Mum at weekends and during the holidays."

Why Does It Happen?

Kieron is telling his sister Holly why he thinks that their parents are splitting up. There can be lots of reasons why parents split up. They may not love each other in the same way as they used to, or they may meet someone else they want to be with. Whatever the reason, it doesn't mean that they will stop loving you.

Why do they argue all the time?

It's just that Mum and Dad don't love each other like they used to.

But why not? It's not fair. I still love them the same.

▶ Arguing Again!

Parents can argue so much they become very unhappy. They may feel that they should part in order to stop the rows. They may decide that even though divorce or separation is upsetting, in the end it will mean that everyone can be happier.

It's quieter here than at home!

◀ New Partners

One parent may find a new friend they can talk to and get on with better. He or she may choose to live with them instead of your mum or dad. If this happens, you may feel very angry towards your parent's new partner.

▶ Mum Still Loves Him

Sometimes only one parent wants to live away from the other parent. If this is the case, the parent who doesn't want the other one to leave may find it difficult to accept and understand the new situation.

15

It's my turn!

It's not. I was playing first.

Story: It's Not Your Fault

1 Jo and Jim Jones were arguing over a computer game.

2 Their mum heard them arguing. She came in and told them off.

I'm fed up with you both fighting all the time!

We've decided to live apart.

It's because we're always fighting, isn't it?

3 A week later, Mr and Mrs Jones told Jo and Jim that they were splitting up.

Are Mr and Mrs Jones splitting up because Jo and Jim argued?

No, definitely not. Parents who split up do so because they feel unhappy with each other. Mrs Jones was cross with Jim and Jo, but it had nothing to do with the decision to separate from Mr Jones. It is important to remember that you are not to blame for the separation or divorce of your parents.

▶ Who's To Blame?

You may want to blame one of your parents if they split up. But grown-ups often decide together to separate or divorce. Even if it is just one parent's choice, blaming him or her won't help anyone.

▼ I Don't Understand

Sometimes the situation may be very complicated. If you can, try talking to an older brother, sister or grandparent to help you to understand better what is happening.

Is it Mum's fault for working too hard?

...or Dad's for playing so much golf?

Kieron, do you understand why your parents are getting a divorce?

"Holly says it's Mum's fault for shouting at Dad. But it's not fair to blame Mum. Dad shouts at Mum, too. I think they are splitting up because they will be happier if they don't live together. I'll miss Dad but it will be better if the rows stop."

Difficult Feelings

Gabriela is round at Carla's house after school. She is asking Carla how she felt when her parents split up. Like Gabriela and Carla, you might have lots of difficult and confusing feelings if your parents separate or get a divorce.

I hate you!

You may feel very angry.

I got upset when people said nasty things about my mum.

I still feel cross with my mum.

▶ But I Want Them Both

You may feel upset and want your mum and dad to stay together, even if they have been sad. You may feel angry with the parent with whom you live and want to blame him or her for the situation. These feelings are quite natural.

Please come back.

Why is she so unhappy?

◀ Nothing's Changed

After splitting up, one or both of your parents may be sad for a while. This can be hard to understand if they split up to stop being unhappy. It can take time to stop feeling sad.

Why is Dad so mean about Mum? She's my mum and I love her.

▶ In The Middle

Sometimes you may feel caught in the middle between your mum and dad. If this happens, talk to your parents about it. Why not ask them to talk to each other, instead of saying things to you about the other one?

Story: Billy's Anger

1 Billy was angry that his parents were splitting up. He didn't want them to.

2 At school, Billy wouldn't do what his teacher asked him to do.

3 Billy told his teacher that he felt as if nobody cared about his feelings.

Why did Billy misbehave at school?

Billy was feeling unhappy and angry. He wanted somebody to take notice of his feelings. But Billy didn't have to misbehave in order to get attention. He could have told his parents or his teacher how he felt. It is better to talk about your feelings, rather than getting cross or even getting into trouble.

Why do they still argue?

▶ Why Isn't It OK Now?

Sometimes your mum and dad may argue, even if they don't live together anymore. It can take time for them to sort out how to share the things they used to own together. They may also still feel cross with each other.

▼ Other People

Sometimes other people don't understand the situation and may say upsetting things about your parents. However hard it is, try to ignore such comments. Instead, chat to good friends and other members of your family. They will understand what is going on.

Carla, how do you cope with your difficult feelings?
"I still feel a bit angry with my mum but I feel better about it now. It was good talking to Gabriela, even though I know it won't make Mum and Dad get back together again."

Feeling OK

Getting used to changes in the family is not easy. Here Kiko is talking to her school nurse about how she feels. When her dad moved out, Kiko really missed him. But she prefers it now because both her parents are happier. It took a while to get used to all the changes.

Friends can make you feel better.

Are things at home better now?

Yes, but it took ages for us to get used to all the changes after Dad left.

▶ In Touch

If you miss your mum or dad, why not write him or her a letter or draw a picture? It may not always be possible to see him or her, but there is nothing wrong in wanting to keep in touch with your other parent.

◀ No Change

Sometimes you have to accept a situation, even though it may not be what you want. If you talk to your parent about your feelings, he or she will be able to understand how you feel about the situation.

▶ Talking Helps

When parents separate or divorce, there will be lots of changes. For instance, you may spend your birthday with only one parent instead of both parents. But just because things are not the same as before doesn't mean that they can't be just as good or even better.

Story: Staying Friends

1 Lucy's mum and dad had split up. Lucy didn't want to see or talk to her mum.

2 Lucy's dad tried to understand why Lucy was so cross with her mum.

3 Lucy's dad persuaded Lucy to talk to her mum. It made her feel better.

Why did Lucy feel better after she had talked to her mum?

Lucy was upset that her mum had left her dad. Speaking to her mum on the telephone didn't make all of her cross and upset feelings go away, but she was glad she had spoken to her mum. A divorce or separation is upsetting for everyone, but bit by bit, sad feelings do go away as you get used to a new situation.

▶ It's OK To Feel Happy

If one or both of your parents are feeling sad you may think that you shouldn't enjoy yourself. It may take a while for your parents to feel OK again, but that doesn't mean that they don't want you to have fun.

◀ It's OK To Feel Sad

If your parents split up, you may feel very confused and unhappy. Hiding your feelings can make everything seem even worse. It helps to talk to friends whose parents have also split up or to a close friend whom you trust.

Kiko, what helped you to feel OK?

"When Mum and Dad separated, I felt lonely so I told my best friend at school. When I felt unhappy, she and my other friend cheered me up. It helped, too, to keep doing the things I always did before, like playing in the basketball team."

Don't Forget...

1

What is your advice to someone whose parents are splitting up, Carla?

"Talk to your parents about your angry or sad feelings, and any other feelings, too! Then your mum and dad will understand better how you feel. Talk to teachers and friends, too. It's not easy, but you do begin to feel better after a while."

2

Was it hard for you when your parents split up, Kieron?

"Yes, but I also understood how it made my parents feel. They didn't want to make me sad. Mums and dads have to sort out what is right for them and for you, even if that means that you may all feel upset for a while. If your parents do separate or get a divorce, they are still your mum and dad. Nothing can change that."

3

Did it take you long to feel better, Kiko?

"Quite a long time. Sometimes I still miss seeing my dad every day, but it's much better now because there is no more shouting. I think it helps to keep doing the things that you usually do, like playing with friends or visiting your favourite places."

4

How do you feel about not seeing your dad, Adam?

"It was really hard at first, but I'm not going to let it stop me from having a good time, because that wouldn't help mum either. I quite like it now, with just me and mum. And lots of friends, too!"

Find Out More About Divorce

Helpful Addresses and Phone Numbers

Talking about problems can really help. If you can't talk to someone close to you, then try ringing one of these organisations:

Childline
Tel: 0800 1111
A 24-hour free helpline for children. The number won't show up on a telephone bill.

Coping with Family Change
PO Box 40, Ashington, NE63 8YR
Tel: 01670 813470
A free multimedia package that gives useful tips on coping with family changes such as when parents split up or new partners arrive.

NSPCC (National Society for the Prevention of Cruelty to Children)
Tel: 0808 800 500
Asian helpline: 0800 096 7719
A 24-hour free helpline offering counselling and practical advice for young people.

Parentline Plus
Tel: 0808 800 2222
A 24-hour free helpline offering counselling and support to parents on many issues, including divorce.

Kids Helpline, Australia
Tel: 1800 55 1800
A 24-hour free helpline for children. Also online help: www.kidshelp.com.au

On the Web

These websites are also helpful. You can get in touch with some of them using email:

www.itsnotyourfault.org

www.nspcc.org.uk

www.divorceaid.co.uk

www.relate.org.uk

www.kidshelp.com.au

www.parentlink.act.gov.au

www.relationships.com.au

www.i-dont.com.au

Further Reading

If you want to read more about divorce and separation, try:

How Can I Deal With: My Parents' Divorce by Sally Hewitt (Franklin Watts)

Choices and Decisions: When Parents Separate by Pete Sanders and Steve Myers (Aladdin/Watts)

Two Homes by Claire Masurel (Candlewick Press)

What Can I Do?: A Book for Children of Divorce by Danielle Lowry and Bonnie J. Matthews (Magination Press)

Help! A Girl's Guide to Divorce and Stepfamilies by Nancy Holyoke (Pleasant Company Publications)

Index

Photocredits

l-left, r-right, b-bottom, t-top, c-centre, m-middle

All photos from istockphoto.com except: Cover tc, 24, 27, 28tl — DAJ.

3, 11, 14, 15, 18, 28bl — Digital Vision. 5, 9 , 13— Brand X Pictures.

All the photos in this book have been posed by models.